From the Pews

DIVINE REVELATIONS FROM THE
MOUTHS OF GOD'S SERVANTS

JEANETTE MARY MAGDALENE
MARK JEROME

Published by: Mary Magdalene House of Peace
Address: 2647 Gateway Rd, Suite 105 #570
Carlsbad, CA 92009   Phone:760-814-2733

Email: info@marymagdalenehouseofpeace.com
Website: marymagdalenehouseofpeace.com

First Edition: February 14, 2020
Original Copyright © 2020: Dr. Jeanette Mary Magdalene

TABLE OF CONTENTS

Preface

This book is a compilation of quotes collected during various sermons attended by the authors over the years. These pages are meant to encourage meditation on these words as spoken by this assemblage of devoted servants of God who were truly inspired by the Holy Spirit. They are organized by topic and grouped into similar thoughts. Each page contains space for the reader to record their own observations, thoughts and meditations.

MARK JEROME
JANUARY 1, 2020
FEAST OF MARY, MOTHER OF GOD

Faith

- Faith is precisely the opening of one's mind, one's understanding to God revealing Himself...

- Faith enables us to connect to God directly...

- Faith involves a continuing effort of personal appropriation and understanding...

- Faith is being able to live and accept unanswered questions...not having all the answers...

- The Faith contains mysteries because the unusual and unfamiliar naturally arouse a keen interest while familiarity breeds contempt...

- The Secrets will not be understood by the uninitiated....one must receive grace to understand...

- Some say "Seeing is believing" ...Jesus said "Believing is seeing" (Jn 2:29)...

- Let us not take for granted that which has been presented to us for conversion...

- One needs a key to see inside prophecies and parables...and that key is FAITH...

- Faith is the "opiate" that allows us to escape the world...but in a supernatural way without a "crash"...

- Faith allows us to somehow already possess that which is to come in the future...

- Do not fear, but walk in faith...

- To "Walk in Faith" (2 Cor 5:7) means moving toward Christ in everything we do...

- Complacency is not the road to travel if we are committed to our Faith...

- Within God's Great Realm there are some things we can grasp by reason alone, while there are other things in God's Treasure that are only known by Faith, although it is not out of our reason...

- The practice of Faith should never be a burden...it should be a Joy...

- Be ready to give an explanation of our Faith...

- "Disciple" means listening from the heart...

- Faith is believing absolutely everything God has revealed...

- To 'Reveal' is to remove the veil...what was always there we will now be able to see...

- Faith frees us from the physical to transcend into and function in the metaphysical and spiritual world...

- Without Faith our knowledge is stunted...

- It takes Faith to put one's finger into a Divine Flame...knowing we will not be burned...

- Jesus would prefer Faith over Theology...(love over reason...)...

- What God reveals is received or seen according to our present capacity...

- Metaphysical is out of this world...ie NOT physical...Faith is required to function in the metaphysical world...

- Much of the metaphysical world remains a mystery...Faith is needed to accept the mystery...and will eventually lead you to the understanding of the mystery...

- Hold fast to God's promises even though their meaning seems hidden...walk by Faith and not by sight (2 Cor 5:7)...

- Jesus did not want the proclamation of who He was to be out of fear...as with the demons (Lk 4:35)...but out of FAITH...as with the disciples...(Mt 16:15-16)

- The devil and his demons are Theological Experts (Mk 5:7)...but without FAITH!

- How can you explain what you SEE in faith to those who are spiritually blind?

- The moment you grow lukewarm everything is a big effort and you willingly encounter distractions from without...but as soon as you begin to conquer yourself and walk uprightly in the Way of God...then the effort expended seems little which before you thought INSURMOUNTABLE...

- Even those seeds that fall in the best soil may still be lost (Lk 8:8)...we must always work for our Faith...

- The world is a dichotomy...people need proof of God while believing all sorts of nonsense...

Truth

- Those who seek the TRUTH are already seeking GOD whether they know it or not...for GOD IS TRUTH...

- The Truth is still the Truth no matter how few believe it while a lie is still a lie no matter how many believe it...*Bishop Fulton Sheen*

- The voice with which Jesus calls us is the TRUTH...

- We do not invent new truths...but we must pass on those established as TRUTH....

- Live only in the Truth of Divine Love...which is the embrace of His Commandments...

- Charity without TRUTH is just sentimentality...

- Christianity is living in the TRUTH...it is how we relate to those around us...let our lamps burn brightly...

- Tell the Truth about yourself in front of God...

- Being humble is to live in the Truth...

- Are we fearless champions of Truth and Justice...?

- Do we seek to silence the Truth or seek repentance for our faults...?

- If the Truth is to set us free...why are we so adverse to it?

- Welcome the Truth and embrace change and conversion...

- Truth sometimes comes from unexpected places...

- Pilate asked Jesus "What is Truth?" (Jn 18:38)...but did not wait for an answer...leading to the Truth of the Cross...

- Truth stirs up hatred in those who don't believe while it brings love and unity to those who do...

- Stand firm in the Truth...protect our hearts with justice...

Theology

- The Bible begins with the Passion of our Lord Jesus Christ and makes more sense when read backwards…

- In the Old Testament it says "Thus says the LORD GOD…"
- In the New Testament Jesus says "Amen, Amen I say to you…"

- The Word of GOD comes to us when we observe IT…

- We don't have a promise of an easier life…we have the promise of Eternal Life (1 John 2:25)…

- The call of God and the refusal to heed fills the Old Testament...but God continues to call...He sent Jesus...but the call is always the same...to REPENT...

- The Old Testament showed us our sins, but gave us no resolutions...The New Testament gave us the Sacraments...

- The letter represents the Old Testament pointing out our faults while the Spirit in the New Testament gives life through the Sacraments...

- The letter kills or condemns while the Spirit gives life...

- The Law was originally written on stone in the 10 Commandments...and then the Word was robed in flesh as Jesus...

- We are meant to walk in the Light and not the realm of Darkness (Jn 12:35)...for those who do not come into the Light prefer the darkness of doubt, fear and sin...

- "Interpret the signs of the times" (Mt 16:3)...to be able to understand the present day happenings through the eyes of God...

- Knowledge is acquired by study whereas Wisdom is acquired by God's inspiration...

- At the Transfiguration (Mt 17:1-13, Mk 9:3-13, Lk 9:28-36)...Moses represents the LAW...the means to live God's way...while Elijah represents the PROPHETS...those speaking for God as people fell away...Jesus, The WORD made flesh...represents the LAW and the PROPHETS...

- The Transfiguration gives a glimpse of God's Glory veiled by flesh...

- We can see ourselves in every instance in every parable...therefore the parable speaks clandestinely to our hearts...

- Doctrine is kept in silence...proclamation is for the whole world...one form of silence is the obscurity used in Scripture making doctrine difficult to understand for the reader...

- Heaven meets earth in the physical church building...

- A steppingstone to Heaven is the Church...

- If I were trying to please man, I would not be a servant of Christ Jesus (Gal 1:10)...

- The wisest thing we can do while on Earth is to SEEK GOD...

- Wisdom is that we COME from GOD and must RETURN to GOD...

- Wisdom is processing facts and information while grounded in GOD...

- How can you tell when the silver is purified....? All the impurities are removed by fire so you can see your reflection in it...so it is with God...once our all our impurities are removed others can see God in us...

- "Fishers of men" (Mt 4:19, Mk 1:17)...catching men into a new life...this "catching" begins at Baptism...but let God "catch us" up into this new life at every Mass through the Gospel and the Eucharist ....

- We must cultivate our vines (Jn 15:2)...for if we leave them to grow on their own, they become tangled in on themselves...they may produce roses...but not so beautiful...grapes...but sour ones...

- Our vines need to be trained to grow out and be exposed to the light...pruned and disciplined...showing the beauty of what God intends...

- God created the Spirits and then matter...and then Spirit within matter...(man)...

- Live as "Children of the Light" (Jn 12:36) because there is so much darkness and ignorance around us...

- Do not mistake Wisdom and Knowledge...Wisdom is the proper use of Knowledge...Knowledge is information gathered by the senses...Wisdom is using the knowledge in a way that goes beyond the senses...a kind of supernatural use of knowledge...

- True Wisdom accepts that the Universe did not happen as an accident...

- Our final destiny as man is leaving the darkness behind and coming into the light of Christ...

- If one believes and is baptized then he will be saved...however, one must live his belief and his baptism to truly be saved...

- We are all called...but at and to different levels...

- The 'call' is not once for all...but a continuous call...

- Do not act in the desires of your former ignorance (1 Pt 1:14)....

- We are earthen vessels that contain a treasure...as such we can be broken...but the message will live on...

- A miracle is a suspension of natural law...

- Miracles are promoters of credibility...

- The righteous will live on only as a soul...while the wicked will receive their body back to live body and soul in Hell...

- "A great tempest arose..." (Mt 8:24)...but the boat will never sink...even if you are seasick...stay in the boat...

Abba Father

- Even when HE reveals Himself God remains a mystery beyond words...if you understood Him, He would not be God...*St Augustine*

- Nothing is more practical than finding GOD...than falling in love in an absolute and final way...what you are in love with, what seizes your imagination...affects everything...

- The present moment is where we meet GOD...

- We are formed with a "GOD-shaped" void within our being...

- In the end we will have no joy at all except in the Glory of GOD...

- Give up everything that does not lead to God....

- The Love of God should be our ultimate goal in all we do...the desire to be with Him always...

- God does not command the impossible from us...

- So many have experienced GOD in a specific way...but have said "NO"...

- There is an evil zeal that separates us from GOD...conversely there is a Just Zeal that brings us closer to GOD...

- We can ask GOD to remove our faults...but in HIS infinite Wisdom HE allows them to remain...

- GOD draws straight with crooked lines...

- Dependence on God gives Him all the Glory...

- May God give us courage to do His Will in all circumstances...

- God does not want your ability...He wants your availability...

- God does not choose the perfect...He perfects those He has chosen...

- Do the work of God and you forget the god of work...

- If we do not try all our lives...God may not be "well pleased" (Mt 3:17)...

- Divest of everything that keeps us from God...

- Choose God and all will be good...follow His Commandments to attain Eternal Life...

- Through Original Sin we have lost the grace to know God...however God incessantly wants/tries to reveal Himself to us...

- In the beginning God often reveals Himself through POWER...but He really wants us to know Him as a gentle, loving God...

- God is always talking to us...we must listen...

- God is always guiding us...instructing us...

- The greatest desire must be that God may always be Glorified in you...

- When God calls AND is heard...He truly gives all that is needed to fulfill that call...

- God wants us to be His instruments...giving us what we need when we need it...

- God frequently gives us a nudge...or a rude awakening...because we have often replaced Him with something else...

- God is that of which no greater thing can be perceived...

- God's gifts are not part of a registry...they are a surprise...

- We can imagine an All Powerful God...but HE is greater than all we can imagine...

- If we do not understand the peace and holiness from God...we must search ourselves...

- God is a Holy Fire that refines us...burning away our sins...

- Without God...we have no purpose...

- There is nothing we can give God that He has not given us first...

- God is in no hurry...His Story spans many centuries...

- There is a God and He desires to reveal hidden and secret things to us...

- Free will...we can choose to love God or not to serve...

- In our life we must strive to not just to know OF God...but to KNOW God...

- No human being is ever lost to God...

- God works all the time...whether we see it or not...

- Act as if all depended on you, while knowing and realizing it all depends on God...

- Cast all your cares on God because He cares for you...

Jesus Christ

- Jesus is God's own self portrait...using the medium of Flesh and Blood...

- Jesus came to remind us that we were created in the image and likeness of God...

- Jesus' purpose was to reveal the Love of the Father...

- While we consider Heaven and earth to by physically distant from one another...Heaven and earth come together completely in the perfect union of the Divine with the Body manifested in Jesus Christ Incarnate...

- If we bear the name "Christian"...we should be mistaken for Christ...

- Because we cannot understand God...Jesus tells us in our own language who God is...Christ makes God personal...

- Pay attention to all the encounters we have with Christ...and rejoice in our life with Christ...

- Evangelization is the facilitation of bringing Christ to another...

- "Do whatever He tells you" (Jn 2:5)...and He will perform miracles in YOUR life...

- Jesus said I AM THE TRUTH (Jn 14:6)...He did not say "I AM the custom"...

- Jesus...use me today....whether I see the results or not is up to you...

- The Father left the house in Heaven (through Jesus) to bring in His wandering and fallen children (the Prodigal Sons)(Lk 15:11)...

- Jesus said..."Do you also want to leave?" (Jn 6:67)...These are not times of peace in the Church or the world...do you want to leave...? But Simon Peter answered Him, "Lord, to whom shall we go? You have the words of eternal life." (Jn 6:68)

- Jesus defeated the devil with His Hands and Feet nailed fast...*St Augustine*

- The Good Shepherd means HE is the ONLY Shepherd (Jn 10:11)...

- If the sheep are not constantly watched by the Shepherd ...they might wander off to pastures that look greener to the sheep....

- A Christian is another Christ...

- The fact that Jesus took on our humanity dignifies our humanity as good...

- The wounds now gush with Divine Mercy...

- As Christ turns to the Cross, HE asks us to turn into little children...

- Christ's sacrifice on the Cross was not for all...for not all will accept it...

- The Galileans shouted "Hosanna" on Palm Sunday (Jn 12:13, Mt 21:9, Mk 11:9)...The Pharisees, Scribes and Jews of Jerusalem shouted "Crucify Him" (Jn 19:15, Mt 27:23, Mk 15:14, Lk 21:23) one week later...

- Follow the obedience of Jesus Who was obedient even to death on a Cross (Php 2:8)...

- All human life is valuable because Jesus was willing to pay the greatest price for it...with His OWN life...

- True Freedom of Christ...willing to sacrifice your life for Freedom as a 'victim soul'...

- If Christ is to increase in me Self must decrease...

- You have been granted the privilege not only to believe in Christ, but to suffer for His Sake...

- We must patiently persevere with Christ...

- We want to save Christ from the cross...but from the Cross Christ saves us...

- On the cross Jesus gave up HIS SPIRIT when He died (Mt 27:50, Lk 23:46, Jn 19:30)...then when He appeared to the Apostles following the Resurrection Jesus breathed on them...telling them to receive the Holy Spirit (Jn 20:22)...

- By coming into the world, Jesus does not seek to set the Spiritual against the physical...for His Birth unites the Spiritual with the Physical...

- Until Christ returns, we will undergo hardship and sin...

- Christ came to show us the Truth about the ways of God...

- We have all come up against things that are hard to believe...("This is hard...who can accept it? Jn 6:60)...it was a way of choosing sides...Jesus already knew who would believe and who would not...their faith was weak and conditional...(ie "I believe as long as you do not ask me to do something difficult...")...

- The deeper we enter into Christ...God's Word...the more there is to know...

- Life without our Lord is occasion for becoming disgruntled for all of us...

- Christ deals with His enemies through irony and parables...

- Look for Christ's Kingship through the eyes of Faith...

- The proof that Christ reigns is that they never cease attacking Him and His Mystical Body...

- Christ has ways of doing things...sometimes appearing like a lamb who was slain...

Holy Spirit

- Just as the soul is the life of the body...the Holy Spirit is the life of the soul...

- It is the Spirit that gives life while the flesh is of no avail (Jn 6:63)...

- It is our responsibility as Christians to listen and respond to the Holy Spirit...

- We cannot come to know Jesus on our own but need the Holy Spirit...

- The Communion of God's Truth with human truth is the Holy Spirit...

- Man is not able to love adequately on his own...he needs the Holy Spirit...

- When we allow our eyes to be opened by the Holy Spirit...it allows us to properly see the "signs of the times" (Mt 16:3)...

- It is impossible without the Holy Spirit...ask constantly for the Holy Spirit...

- The Church is not without sinners, but it is without sin...The Holy Spirit guarantees that...

- The Holy Spirit is to the Church what the soul is to the body...

- When considering travel by boat...the oars are Virtue and can move us, but raise the sails...those Gifts of the Holy Spirit...and the Holy Spirit will move us much faster...

Trinity

- We pray TO The FATHER...THROUGH the SON...IN the HOLY SPIRIT...

- The most important thing in life is timing, timing, timing...the timing of the Father, the timing of the Son and the timing of the Holy Spirit...

Kingdom of God

- The Kingdom of God is not just at the end...it is the whole journey of our life on Earth...

- God the Father has given us the Kingdom through Jesus His Son...

- If one rejects the Word of God...he rejects the Kingdom of God...

- The Word of God is so deep and has so many layers that the Kingdom of God is not clearly defined by any one word...

- The Kingdom of God is now...The Kingdom of Heaven is FOREVER...

- The Kingdom of God grows with man's help...but he knows not how...

- May our lives become a parable that says...'Thy Kingdom come, Thy Will be done' (Mt 6:10)...

- God asks us to throw out His Seed...and He will water it...

- Each of us will be challenged by the Kingdom of God in our own way...

- The Kingdom of God versus The Kingdom of Heaven...The Kingdom of Heaven is that state of perfect happiness...The Kingdom of God is what we must constantly seek after in this life...it is the earthly application...we need to live it...for "the Kingdom of God is at hand" (Mk 1:15)...

- Jesus said..."know that the Kingdom of God is at hand. Amen I say to you, this generation shall not pass away until all things be fulfilled." (Lk 21:31-32)...Jesus, by His Life, Death and Resurrection, brought the Kingdom of God among us...

- "My Kingdom is not of this world" (Jn 18:36)...Jesus' Power is as mighty and hidden today as it was then...

- We are born in the sin of Adam and Eve...then baptized out of it...then influenced by the sin around us...Jesus comes to call us back to HIM...back to the Kingdom of God...living daily for God...laboring constantly against sin to reach Heaven...

- What Is the Kingdom of God? It is eventually Paradise...mankind locked himself out of Paradise by sin...by repenting and believing in the Gospel, man was let back in...

Love

- Let love be the focus of all we do...

- Love is not complete unless it is given away and shared...

- We must remain in Jesus' love because only God can love perfectly...

- Love one another...not in a carnal way...but as Jesus loves...

- Today God is loving the world through us...

- Love is total dignity and respect for others...we as human beings have lost the LOVE....

- It is easier to be obedient than it is to love...obedience comes from the will while love comes from the heart...

- Do small things with great love...St Therese of Lisieux

- The practical application of Charity is the most potent....

- If we cannot control our tongue...our religion is in vain...

- Do good...but do it with a good attitude...

- If we are to be role models it is not enough to do good...we must BE good...

- Love built solely on emotion is like a house built on sand...love based on rock is from God...

- The definition of True Christian Love is wanting the best for someone no matter the circumstances...

Humility

- Humility is doing everything with a deep love for God...

- Humility is seeing ourselves as exactly who we are, no more and no less...

- What you are before God is what you are...

- Humility is true self-knowledge...

- Only through humility will Jesus reveal the Truth...

- Put on humility as the first step...

- True humility means you depend totally on God and not on ourselves...

- True humility is when we cast our worries on God because He loves us...

- It is good for us to run into opposition and have others think badly of us even when our intentions are good...for these things help us to be humble and rid us of our pride...then we seek God more earnestly...

- We are often too full of ourselves and need to be more humble and more obedient...

- Lord, if you want me, please help me...

- Obedience means to listen more intently...

- Swallow your pride...it is not fattening...

- Humility is truly seeing ourselves in the way God sees us...

- It is critical to be known by God...

- What is important is to serve...do not worry whether it is the first place or the last place...

- Do not be anonymous...but serve in the capacity in which you find yourself...

- How generous you are is a measure of how humble you are...

- Humility takes reality checks...

- We must live out a virtue of silence...so we can hear God and hear others...

- The more you know the more severely you will be judged...so do not be proud of any skill or knowledge you have...for such is an awesome responsibility...

- Sometimes we must be empty in order to receive...

- We may never come to something new if we are afraid of emptiness...

Grace

- The protection of God is His Grace...

- It is not all about our efforts...but about God's Grace....

- God's grace is there if we wait for wisdom and prudence...

- God often reminds us that HE loved us first...although we do not merit His Grace and Blessings...

- Pray daily for the Grace of final perseverance...

- Pray for the Grace to carry our crosses daily...

- It is only by God's Grace...through prayer and sacraments...that the Scriptures are opened to us...

- Without God's Grace there will be no conversion...

- Man cannot have one good thought or work meritorious of Heaven without God's Grace...

- Perform daily actions in a state of Grace...

- One cannot even say "Jesus Christ my LORD and GOD" without God's Grace...

- May God's Grace go before us AND follow us...

- How many times do you have to "die" in order to experience Grace in your life...

- Grace builds in knowledge...

- Rejoice in your rejections for He gives you strength to go on in His Grace...

- Jesus is the sower (Lk 8:5)...He plants the seeds and cultivates them with GRACE...

- We must cut down on our needs by receiving God's Grace...

- It takes more strength and maturity to have mercy than bitterness and resentment...

- We do not merit the Grace of a Holy Death...we must pray for it...

- Do not accept God's Grace in vain...

Peace

- True Christian peace is the ability to cope with the tension and conflict which is inescapable in this human life...

- You must have peace within...because you cannot give what you do not have...

- Being peaceful is an act of charity...

- From Charity comes peace...despite all the trials and tribulations of life...

- The world has enough "hand wringers"...we must use our creativity and imagination to change it...

- Peace is tranquility of order...he who has God on his side fears nothing...

- Only a strong person can be gentle...a weak person must be aggressive and defensive...

- While socialism or even communism might be a great theory, it requires perfect people...and the world has always had a shortage of those...

Hope

- Hope is a Gift from God where we look forward to Heaven...

- Our Hope does not depend on proving man has a spiritual nature...

- Let us see each mountain or hill we encounter...not as an obstacle...but as a steppingstone...

- Always be prepared to mount a defense of the hope you have...

Prayer

- Prayer is cyclical...there is inspiration from God to pray...and the prayer goes back to God from us...

- Pray that we never confuse the purifying fires of Heaven with the destructive fires of hell...

- If the only prayer you ever said in your life was "Thank You"...that would be enough...

- Our prayer is that we let God speak to us...for God speaks to us continuously but we are not often tuned to his frequency...

- 'Our Father' (Mt 6:9, Lk 11:2) and 'Hail Mary' (Lk 1:28) are Heavenly Words...

- We chose the road we take in Faith and Prayer...is it wrapped up in ourselves or completely immersed in God...praising and thanksgiving...

- When praying, raise your heart and mind to the Lord even if dry or distracted...Love the prayer...make everything a sacrifice...

Christmas

- Christmas...the day of our salvation....

- God and sinner reconciled...

- God becoming man was the manifestation of His love for us....

- God has come to save us that we might live in the light and not the darkness...

- Before the birth of Christ, man could not experience God's love firsthand...

- To live without the Christ Child is to live in a state of darkness...

- The Christ Child is innocence, simplicity and love...

- Unless you acknowledge the gravity of your sinful state, you will never experience the TRUE JOY of Christmas!

- Christmas is Jesus' Birthday, but He brings the gifts...

- When shepherds had an unblemished lamb they wrapped it in swaddling bandages to keep it from bruising and laid it in a manger to protect it from the other lambs and keep it unblemished...this was the sign conveyed to the shepherds from the angel of the Lord at the Nativity...that Jesus would be wrapped in swaddling clothes and lying in a manger (Lk 2:12)...this was a foreshadowing of Christ as the Pascal Lamb...but also lying in a manger as Food from Heaven...

Easter

- We know good always triumphs even in the face of evil because Good Friday leads to Easter Sunday...

- The resurrection of Jesus Christ is the visible sign of the invisible victory of the Cross...

- (Doubting) Thomas the Apostle knew that the Savior must have 5 wounds....(Unless I see the marks of the nails in His Hands and put my hand in His side, I will not believe" Jn 20:25)

- The Resurrection is an eruption of light...

- We are called to be "Easter People" throughout the year…People of Light…

- The Resurrection is the visible sign of the invisible victory on the Cross…

- If we carry our cross joyfully out of love of God and love of man…then we can rejoice in our own resurrection…

- The cross must be completely embraced if the disciple is to experience the absolute victory…

- God' Communion with us is the Cross…

- On Easter Night Jesus did three things: He showed them His Wounds (the Body)...He breathed on them (the Spirit)...and He instituted Forgiveness (Jn 20:20-23)...Body, breath, sin...In Genesis ...God formed man from the earth (Gn 2:7)...Jesus rose from the earth (Mt 28:6)...God breathed spirit into man (Gn 2:7)...Jesus breathed the Holy Spirit onto His disciples (Jn 20:22)...man sinned against God in the Garden of Eden (Gn 3:1-7)...Jesus instituted Forgiveness of sins (Jn 20:23)...A New Beginning for the Human Race...

- When Jesus appears to the disciples after the Resurrection, He does not feed them with His own fish but asks them to bring their own catch (Jn 21:9)...He does provide them with His bread...(Jn 21:13)...

- Once Peter has been 'fed'...he can hear our Lord..."Do you Love me?" (Jn 21:15)...

- Three times Peter denied our Lord (Mt 26:69-75)...three times our Lord asked Peter if he loved Him (Jn 21:15-17)...total forgiveness...forgiveness three times is forgiveness by the Trinity...

Eucharist

- All gifts are a symbol of love...except the Eucharist...which is LOVE ITSELF...

- The Eucharist opens the Kingdom of God to us...

- The Kingdom of God is at hand in the Eucharist at every Mass...

- The Eucharist brings us into contact with Jesus' Divinity...

- At every Mass the Crucifixion is multiplied among us...

- We often fail to reap the benefit of the Mass...therefore attend many Masses...

- Adam and Eve tried to EAT their way to God and thereby lost their standing with God by introducing sin (Gn 3:1-7)...Jesus restores us and brings us back to God by giving us His Flesh to EAT (Jn 6:53-57)...

- We unite with Christ's Love in the Eucharist...

- The Eucharist is supernatural holiness received every time...

Sacraments

- Confession is not a judgement, but a meeting with the Father...

- 'Repent' does not always mean to say you are sorry...but to change your life...

- The world does not want us to find a solution...but God does...

- Through Baptism we are no longer descended from Adam...but from Christ...

- Lack of forgiveness is one of the biggest obstacles to Holiness...

- Confession without conversion will not lead to salvation...

- If our Soul is neglected, we will be unable to work in any part of God's vineyard...

Holy Mother Church

- If we are to be deeply rooted in Christ...we must plant ourselves in the Church...

- At times we may feel spiritually dormant...but we must remain planted in His Orchard...The Church...trimmed clean through the sacrament of Penance...

- It is ours to do something prophetic with our lives...

Holy Mother of God

- We pray THROUGH Mary to GOD...

- Not Jesus or Mary...but Jesus AND Mary...

- Christ's first miracle was brought about by the prayers of His Mother Mary at Cana...He wanted to be asked by her (Jn 2:1-11)...

- Experience Christ's Passion through the tears of the Blessed Virgin...

- When we do the Will of God we are like Mary...bringing Jesus into the world...

- Imitate the Blessed Virgin Mary...her most noble trait, "Fiat", "Let it be done to me" (Lk 1:38), opened the door to her most admirable trait, Mother of God...submitting to the Will of the Father conquers evil...it brought the Word Incarnate...it brought God to earth for the salvation of all..."FIAT" vs "Non Serviam!" (I will not serve!)...

Holy Family

- St Joseph...was sanctified in the womb...given grace at birth...and lived without concupiscence...

- The Holy Family lived in obedience to God...Jesus came to do the Father's will...Mary gave her *fiat* and remained a perpetual virgin...Joseph accepted his wife and Jesus as his adopted son...The Holy Family had supernatural grace bestowed upon them but still had free will...they chose to obey God...we received supernatural graces at Baptism but still need to choose to live a Holy life...

- Jesus could have grown up without parents...but chose to grow up in a human family...

Church Militant

- Being Christian does not necessarily mean we are to triumph in this world…

- If you do not "take up your Cross and follow Me" (Mk 8:34)…you are not Christian…

- Live in the world, but do not be of the world (2 Cor 10:3)….

- God guarantees us that the Church will always endure (Mt 16:18), but not necessarily that we will always be part of it…we have free will…

- If we follow Christ, we will be rejected in this life...

- Being a witness to God is being rejected by society...

- Do not seek to be known on earth....rather be known in Heaven...

Good vs Evil

- Evil is ever present...if one is not filled with good then evil will take over...

- There cannot be a state of indifference...we choose FOR God or evil...

- Know the opponent...the world, the flesh and the devil...

- Human beings possess greatness because they can choose to do good or evil...Pope John Paul II

- Human life is lived between good and evil…. Pope John Paul II

- God allows evil to bring us back to HIM…

- Pray for the grace to resist the devil and all our stupidity…

- Evil can never speak the Truth…

- Man's "steady-state" always gravitates toward evil…therefore one must always strive to overcome sin…this takes constant energy to overcome the "steady-state"…

- Vigilance implies that there IS an enemy against whom we must remain vigilant...

- There is no denying this fact...there IS an enemy...

- God allows evil to exist to test us...for there can be no crown without a victory...and no victory without a fight...

- The 'Gates of the Netherworld will not prevail against (the Church)' (Mt 16:18)...meaning that the Church must attack against hell and conquer it...we must join in the fight against evil...

- God always works toward unity...while the devil works against it...

- Jesus did not allow the demons to speak in the Gospel accounts because they knew who He WAS...but did not KNOW Him...

- Jesus defeated the devil and his demons with His Hands and Feet nailed fast...(St. Augustine)

- The devil never sleeps...nor is the flesh dead yet...therefore always be prepared to do battle for you are surrounded by enemies that never rest...

- If your heart is full of love for Jesus...there is no room there for demons...

- Demons are in a state of perpetual hatred...they burn with hatred for man and therefore serve as purification for those who are able to withstand their temptations...

- We become slaves of the devil when we forget he exists...we become proud when we forget that God exists...

- When we worry, we are fighting God and giving in to the devil...

- In the face of demonic attacks...pray, be faithful and be prophetic...being prophetic means declaring the TRUTH and proclaiming the Word of God...

- Regardless of the evil in the world...we are asked to place our trust in Jesus...

- It is a sharp, two edged sword discerning good from evil...

- Our weapon cannot be the same as that against which we are fighting...we cannot fight evil with evil...

- "Be not overcome by evil, but overcome evil by good." (Ro 12:21)…"Noli vinci a malo sed vince in bono malum".

- The devil seeks to remove our Graces…

- Evil is lurking at your door…resist him…

Suffering

- When a Christian does not suffer any difficulties in life...something is wrong...you cannot remove the cross from Christ...

- Christian life is a combat...a war without mercy...

- The Way to Heaven is the Cross..."Via Dolorosa"...

- If all goes well on earth, how can you expect to be crowned in Heaven for a patience you never practiced?

- God frees us from strife, not by making our troubles disappear, but by helping us not to be overcome by suffering...

- Suffering in life is a good thing because it is God asking us to accept HIS WILL and be part of the Holy Family...

- Our pain and suffering is allowed by God to tell us that there is a God waiting for us...

- Pain and suffering can end in Glory...

- If we trust in God even when we suffer...we will be at peace...

- God is not the author of suffering...He is ultimately on our side...

- All the trials we experience in this llfe bring us closer to God...

- Be patient in the face of trials and afflictions...

- Pain is a physiological sign there is something wrong in our bodies...Guilt is a psychological sign there is something wrong in our hearts and souls...

- Passionate investment leaves us vulnerable to loss...

- Falling is not the problem...staying on the ground is...

Sin

- In order to overcome sin two things are necessary...free choice and the Grace of God...

- Pray for a well-formed conscience and to know our main faults so as to avoid sin...

- When our needs are filled easily, we are tempted to move away from God...

- God brought us into existence and yet we sin...altering His plan for us...

- Avoiding sin is passive...but we are asked to be proactive...

- Seek Freedom...but not 'absolute freedom'...giving in to freedom of sin is not Freedom at all...

- Sin decreases the freedom of all...

- Sin is a thief robbing us of sanctifying Grace...

- Everyone who is part of the Body of Christ is tempted without end...

- Temptation is not sin...entertaining temptation will lead to sin...

- Sin did not take away our Glorified State...it only changed and removed our proper perception of it...our perception will return in the Final Judgement...

- We celebrate freedom...but freedom (free will) given by God often results in sin...

- When we rule our passions we do good things..."Be angry, but do not sin" (Ps 4:4)...

- Our past does not dictate our future...

- The Cross is a compass that will guide us to victory over sin and death...

- Few understand how truly terrible sin is...

- Moral Relativism...If everything is good...nothing is good...

Judging Others

- We should never judge another as their behavior may be the result of less Grace or no Grace at all...

- Judgement of others leaves little room for empathy...

- When you see someone that irritates you...pick up the beam... *(Jesus said "How can you say to your brother, 'Let me take the speck out of your eye,' while there is still a beam in your own eye?" Mt 7:3)*

Made in the USA
Columbia, SC
05 March 2020